THE BIG 70

Your Survival Guide

An exclusive edition for

for all your gift books and gift stationery

This edition first published in Great Britain in 2018 by
Allsorted Ltd, Watford, Herts, UK WD19 4BG

© Susanna Geoghegan Gift Publishing

Author: Emma Hill

Cover design: Milestone Creative

ISBN: 978-1-911517-52-8

Printed in China

THE BIG 70 IS UPON YOU!

What to do with the next decade of your life? Firstly, you could dip into this book filled with witticisms, truths, jokes and advice on turning 70. Sure, we can look back on your 50s and 60s with wistful nostalgia; those heady days when standing up wasn't always prefixed with an 'oof', but mostly we're looking ahead with optimism and enthusiasm, comfortable in our own skin, definitely wiser and ready to embark on a later-life adventure. Don't let getting older drag you down (who knows how long it will take you to get back up again), embrace your sensational seventies and let life begin!

YOU KNOW YOU ARE 70 WHEN...

- Standing up takes a while

- You suffix many of your sentences with 'in my day'

- You enjoy hearing about other people's operations

- You fall asleep after one glass of wine

- Your feet become unsightly – corns, bunions, yellowing toenails...

- You wake up with a new pain every morning

- You can't find your reading glasses...when they're on top of your head

- That little old person in the mirror is you

- Your drinks cabinet contains sherry and port – and they're not at the back covered in dust

YOUR CLOTHES ARE CONSIDERED 'VINTAGE'

THESE ARE THE SOUL'S CHANGES. I DON'T BELIEVE IN AGEING. I BELIEVE IN FOREVER ALTERING ONE'S ASPECT TO THE SUN. HENCE MY OPTIMISM.

VIRGINIA WOOLF

A WORD FROM THE WISE

The answer to old age is to keep one's mind busy and go on with one's life as if it were interminable.
Leon Edel

I live in that solitude which is painful in youth, but delicious in the years of maturity.
Albert Einstein

Age is only a number we count until we're old enough to know it doesn't count.
Katrina Mayer

As soon as you feel too old to do a thing, do it!
Margaret Deland

Old age takes away from us what we have inherited and gives us what we have earned.
Gerald Brenan

50s & 60s TRIVIA
(PART 1)

1. Who delivered his 'Wind of Change' speech in 1960?

2. Who played the role of Norman Bates in the 1960 Hitchcock classic **Psycho**?

3. Which Elvis Presley song made Christmas number one in the US in 1962?

4. In April 1960, 60,000 protestors staged a demonstration in London against what?

5. Which five swinging buddies made up the 'Rat Pack'?

6. What toy made its debut at the 1959 New York toy fair?

7. Which well-known board game made its modern day version debut in 1960?

8. Who defeated Richard Nixon to become US president in 1960?

9. What was Elvis Presley's first number one hit?

10. Where did Gerald Durrell open his zoo in 1958?

(See page 94 for answers)

THINGS TO DO NOW YOU'RE 70

- Splurge on something you've always wanted
- Never stop learning
- Have your portrait painted
- Track down a long lost relative
- Retire
- Learn about new technologies
- Talk to strangers in a queue
- Read a classic novel
- Engage in gentle exercise every day

TAKE UP A NEW HOBBY

I BELIEVE MY HOUSE IS HAUNTED. EVERY TIME I LOOK IN MY MIRROR A CRAZY OLD LADY STANDS IN FRONT OF ME SO I CAN'T SEE MY REFLECTION!

UNKNOWN

YOU'RE HAVING A LAUGH

A couple had not been getting along for years, so the husband thinks, 'I'll buy my wife a cemetery plot for her 70th birthday.'
Well, you can imagine her disappointment.
The next year, her birthday rolls around again and this time he doesn't get her anything.
She says, 'Why didn't you get me a birthday present?'
He replies, 'You didn't use what I got you last year!'

Turning 70 is like turning 21 in Celsius

My grandmother was a very tough woman. She buried three husbands and two of them were just napping.
Rita Rudner

When I was a boy the Dead Sea was only sick.
George Burns

JUST WHEN THE CATERPILLAR THOUGHT THE WORLD WAS OVER IT BECAME A BUTTERFLY.

PROVERB

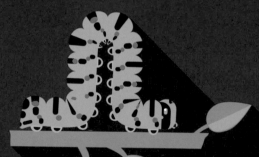

A WORD FROM THE WISE

To be seventy years young is sometimes far more cheerful and hopeful than to be forty years old.
Oliver Wendell Holmes Sr.

I am an old man and have known a great deal of troubles, but most of them never happened.
Mark Twain

Youth is a gift of nature, but age is a work of art.
Stanislaw Jerzy Lec

When grace is joined with wrinkles, it is adorable. There is an unspeakable dawn in happy old age.
Victor Hugo

It takes a long time to become young.
Pablo Picasso

DID YOU KNOW?

The philosopher Immanuel Kant published what are arguably some of his greatest works between the age of 60 and 80. So perhaps it's time to stop worrying about your brain cells shrivelling and your creative capacity diminishing?

The average person will have lost around 105 pounds of skin by 70 years of age.

It is now believed that only about 30 per cent of the characteristics of ageing are genetically determined. The other 70 per cent are linked to lifestyle, so how long you live depends an awful lot on the manner in which you live.

EXERCISE HAS BEEN SHOWN TO PREVENT MEMORY LOSS. EVEN BEING ACTIVE JUST ONCE A WEEK CAN HAVE A POSITIVE IMPACT ON YOUR COGNITIVE FUNCTION, SO GET UP OFF THAT CHAIR AND GET MOVING!

70 THINGS YOU SHOULD KNOW BY THE TIME YOU TURN 70 (PART 1)

- How to laugh at life

- It's never to late too learn something new

- You should retire to something not from something

- Tomorrow isn't guaranteed...so appreciate the time you have

- It's OK to say no

- Happiness is a choice

- How to be kind to yourself

- Death is inevitable...so you must live life to the full

- Success is how you define it

YOU SHOULD GO TO THE TOILET WHENEVER YOU SEE ONE, 'JUST IN CASE'

YOU'RE NEVER TOO OLD

At 72, aviatrix Margaret Ringenberg completed the Round-the-World Air Race.

Ernestine Shepherd began a career as a bodybuilder at the age of 56 and competed well into her 70s.

Sean Connery was knighted by Queen Elizabeth II at the age of 70.

Peter Mark Roget published the Roget's Thesaurus that made him a household name when he was 73.

HARRY TRUMAN RECEIVED AN HONORARY CIVIC LAW DEGREE FROM OXFORD UNIVERSITY AGED 72.

YOU KNOW YOU ARE 70 WHEN...

- You fall asleep in front of the television...

- ...after having complained about how there's nothing but rubbish on television these days

- You've been there, done that...but can't remember what it was

- You've traded in your headphones for hearing aids

- You groan when you bend down to pick something off the floor

- ...and it takes you a while to get back up again

- You take a keen interest in the weather forecast... even when you're not going out

- You go to more funerals than weddings

- You stop halfway through an answer because you can't remember the question

YOU MOVE THE NEWSPAPER IN AND OUT IN AN ATTEMPT TO SEE IT BETTER

IN MY OLD AGE THERE IS A
COMING INTO FLOWER. MY BODY
WANES; MY MIND WAXES.

VICTOR HUGO

A WORD FROM THE WISE

To know how to grow old is the master-work of wisdom, and one of the most difficult chapters in the great art of living.
Henri Frederic Amiel

"You're very old, aren't you?"
"Just as old as my tongue and a little older than my teeth."
Philippa Pearce

What youth deemed crystal, age finds out was dew.
Robert Browning

I was wise enough to never grow up while fooling most people into believing I had.
Margaret Mead

People don't grow old. When they stop growing, they become old.
Unknown

50s & 60s TRIVIA
(PART 2)

1. In which year did the farthing cease to be legal tender?

2. Which film, starring Yul Brynner and Deborah Kerr, was released in June 1956?

3. Who did John F. Kennedy defeat in the US Presidential election race in 1960?

4. Frank Sinatra and who divorced in 1957?

5. What is the brand name of the fabric hook-and-loop fastener that was introduced commercially in the late 50s?

6. Who were the backing singers on most of Elvis Presley's early hits?

7. Which country hosted the 1962 FIFA World Cup?

8. What was the name of the chimp that was sent into space in Project Mercury mission MR-2 in January 1961?

9. Which TV show provided Frankie Laine with a UK top ten hit in 1960?

10. Which toy, imported from Australia, was huge in 1958?

(See page 95 for answers)

THINGS TO DO NOW YOU'RE 70

- Get regular medical check-ups
- Join a discussion group
- Read your way through a book wish list
- Make peace with yourself
- Attend a class, lecture or seminar on something that interests you
- Participate in your local community
- Eat healthy, regular meals
- Join a book club
- Give away something precious

PLAY A MUSICAL INSTRUMENT

AGE DOES NOT DIMINISH THE
EXTREME DISAPPOINTMENT OF
HAVING A SCOOP OF ICE CREAM
FALL FROM THE CONE.
JIM FIEBIG

YOU'RE HAVING A LAUGH

As a senior citizen was driving down the motorway, his car phone rang. Answering, he heard his wife's voice urgently warning him: 'Eric, I just heard on the news that there's a car going the wrong way down the M25. Please be careful!' 'Hell,' said Eric, 'It's not just one car. It's hundreds of them!'

You've heard of the three ages of man – youth, middle age, and 'you're looking wonderful'.
Francis Cardinal Spellman

You know you're getting old when you get that one candle on the cake. It's like, 'See if you can blow this out'.
Jerry Seinfeld

70 THINGS YOU SHOULD KNOW BY THE TIME YOU TURN 70 (PART 2)

- Having fun is the best way to forget your pains
- Age is not a disease
- How to love the simple moments
- How to speak your truth...quietly and clearly
- How to be cheerful in the face of adversity
- You are in charge of what happens next
- How to forgive
- Express your love
- Love...it's all about love

VITAMINS ARE
POINTLESS

THE MORE SAND THAT HAS ESCAPED FROM THE HOURGLASS OF OUR LIFE, THE CLEARER WE SHOULD SEE THROUGH IT.

JEAN-PAUL SARTRE

A WORD FROM THE WISE

If wrinkles must be written upon our brows, let them not be written upon the heart. The spirit should never grow old.
James A. Garfield

I suppose real old age begins when one looks backward rather than forward.
May Sarton

Old age has a great sense of calm and freedom.
Plato

Youth is the time of getting, middle age of improving, and old age of spending.
Anne Bradstreet

Thank goodness for the first snow, it was a reminder - no matter how old you became and how much you'd seen, things could still be new if you were willing to believe they still mattered.
Candace Bushnell

AT 71, KATSUSUKE YANAGISAWA, A RETIRED JAPANESE SCHOOLTEACHER, BECAME THE OLDEST PERSON TO CLIMB MOUNT EVEREST.

YOU'RE NEVER TOO OLD

At 75, Nelson Mandela was elected president of South Africa.

Lord Palmerston became Prime Minister at the age of 71.

At the age of 72, Oscar Swahn became the oldest person to compete in the 1920 Summer Olympics.

Chuck Yeager re-enacted his first breaking of the sound barrier 50 years earlier aged 74.

70 THINGS YOU SHOULD KNOW BY THE TIME YOU TURN 70 (PART 3)

- Time heals many things
- Nobody else controls you
- Worrying is futile
- Hoard time not stuff
- How to be present in the moment
- Every year is a privilege
- How to embrace the little pleasures in the everyday
- To admit your mistakes
- It doesn't matter what other people think of you

SHERRY MAKES DAYTIME DRINKING ACCEPTABLE

A WORD FROM THE WISE

The very old and the very young have something in common that makes it right that they should be left alone together. Dawn and sunset see stars shining in a blue sky; but morning and midday and afternoon do not, poor things.
Elizabeth Goudge

I will never be an old man. To me, old age is always 15 years older than I am.
Francis Bacon

Wear your years with pride, like a badge of honour, for you have conquered. You have thrived. You have survived!
Unknown

What's a man's age? He must hurry more, that's all; Cram in a day, what his youth took a year to hold.
Robert Browning

LIFE IS LIKE A BICYCLE. TO KEEP YOUR BALANCE, YOU MUST KEEP MOVING.

ALBERT EINSTEIN

THINGS TO DO NOW YOU'RE 70

- Play games to keep your mind fresh
- Learn to dance the tango
- Host a fundraiser
- Sing out loud
- Renew an old friendship
- Cook your way through a cookbook
- Visit a wonder of the world
- Apologise
- Learn a magic trick

DRIVE AN OPEN-TOP SPORTS CAR

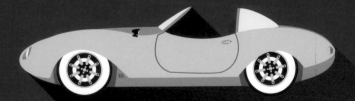

JUST 'CAUSE THERE'S SNOW ON THE ROOF DOESN'T MEAN THERE'S NOT A FIRE INSIDE.

BONNIE HUNT

YOU'RE HAVING A LAUGH

I have achieved my seventy years in the usual way, by sticking strictly to a scheme of life which would kill anybody else... I will offer here, as a sound maxim, this: That we can't reach old age by another man's road.
Mark Twain

Old people really do have a secret though. You wanna know what it is? Luck.
Craig Ferguson

I've still got it, but nobody wants to see it.

May you live to be so old that your family talks about you like you're not even there.

I don't feel old – I don't feel anything until noon. Then it's time for my nap.
Bob Hope

If things get better with age, then I'm approaching magnificent!

AS YOU AGE, YOUR SENSE
OF SMELL AND TASTE CAN
DIMINISH SO YOU MAY FEEL
AN INCREASED NEED TO
SPICE UP YOUR SUPPER!

DID YOU KNOW?

That shrinking feeling isn't an illusion - as you get older your vertebrae compress, causing you to lose around an inch off your height.

A recent study found that people were happiest in youth and then again in their 70s and early 80s, so it's not all downhill...

Inventor of the telephone, Alexander Graham Bell, also set a world water-speed record of over 70 miles an hour at the age of 72. No reason to revert back to speedos at your age, but pretty impressive nonetheless.

70 THINGS YOU SHOULD KNOW BY THE TIME YOU TURN 70 (PART 4)

- Growing old beats the alternative
- You are what you do, not what you say
- How not to over-apologise
- Holding on to something makes it easier to stand up...you'll still say 'oof' though
- Be grateful
- Rest is a valid use of time
- It's OK to be content with being ordinary
- Don't beat yourself up over your mistakes
- You never stop learning

PEACE IS SOMETHING TO STRIVE FOR

MARY WESLEY WROTE TEN BESTSELLERS INCLUDING THE CAMOMILE LAWN AFTER SHE WAS 70.

YOU'RE NEVER TOO OLD

At 75, Barbara Hillary became one of the oldest people, and the first black woman, to reach the North Pole.

At 73, Yeats completed his final play and poems.

Olga Kotelko started training in track and field age 77 and by the time she was 92 held 20 world records.

At 74, Ferdinand Marie de Lesseps began an attempt to construct the Suez Canal.

YOU KNOW YOU ARE 70 WHEN...

- A tablet is something you take to ease the pains, not an electronic gadget

- You tell the same story over and over again

- You talk about your ailments...a lot

- You need an afternoon nap

- You start driving very slowly

- Your ears are noticeably bigger

- You wonder why everyone is mumbling

- You tell yourself teeth are overrated

- Your children look middle-aged

- You tuck tissues up your sleeve when you have a cold

BIRTHDAYS ARE A COUNTDOWN RATHER THAN A CELEBRATION

50s & 60s TRIVIA
(PART 3)

1. Which fashion designer created the miniskirt in 1964?

2. Which single of 1961 provided Petula Clark with her first UK number one?

3. Which South African leader was sentenced to life in prison in 1964?

4. Which 60s artist was famous for his renderings of everyday objects such as soup cans?

5. Which single of 1964 became the Dave Clark Five's first UK number one?

6. In 1964, Terence Conran opened his first of which chain of shops in Fulham Road, London?

7. In 1957, Egypt reopened what?

8. Which band helped springboard the careers of guitarists Eric Clapton, Jeff Beck and Jimmy Page?

9. Which iconic blonde actress was found dead in her bedroom on August 5, 1962?

10. Who directed the 1962 film **Lawrence of Arabia**?

(See page 95 for answers)

WE ARE HAPPIER IN MANY WAYS
WHEN WE ARE OLD THAN WHEN
WE WERE YOUNG. THE YOUNG SOW
WILD OATS. THE OLD GROW SAGE.
WINSTON CHURCHILL

A WORD FROM THE WISE

Age isn't how old you are but how old you feel.
Gabriel García Márquez

When I can look life in the eyes, grow calm and very coldly wise, life will have given me the truth, and taken in exchange my youth.
Sara Teasdale

Whatever a man's age, he can reduce it several years by putting a bright-colored flower in his button-hole.
Mark Twain

It's sad to grow old, but nice to ripen.
Brigitte Bardot

The longer I live the more beautiful life becomes.
Frank Lloyd Wright

THINGS TO DO NOW YOU'RE 70

- Take a photo a day

- Try Tai Chi

- Practice mindfulness

- Master a foreign language

- Listen to your music collection in its entirety

- Drink vintage champagne

- Dye your hair a crazy colour

- Perform with a local amateur dramatics company

- Take care of your body

ADOPT A DOG

YOU CAN'T TURN BACK THE CLOCK...BUT YOU CAN WIND IT UP AGAIN.

YOU'RE HAVING A LAUGH

Three elderly sisters, ages 92, 94 and 96, shared a house together. One evening, the 96-year-old sister went upstairs to take a bath. As she put her foot into the tub, she paused. Then she yelled down to the other two sisters and asked, 'Was I getting in the tub or out?'

'You darn fool,' said the 94-year-old. 'I'll come up and see.' When she got half way up the stairs she paused. 'Was I going up the stairs or down?'

The 92-year-old sister was sitting at the kitchen table drinking a cup of tea and thought, 'I hope I never get that forgetful, knock on wood.' She shook her head and called out, 'I'll be up to help you both as soon as I see who's at the door.'

It is a bad idea to live too long. Few carry it off well.
Charles Frazier

Nice to be here? At my age it's nice to be anywhere.
George Burns

THE SOUL IS BORN OLD BUT GROWS YOUNG. THAT IS THE COMEDY OF LIFE. AND THE BODY IS BORN YOUNG BUT GROWS OLD. THAT IS LIFE'S TRAGEDY.

OSCAR WILDE

A WORD FROM THE WISE

Grow old with me! The best is yet to be.
Robert Browning

I think your whole life shows in your face and you
should be proud of that.
Lauren Bacall

The privilege of a lifetime is to become who you really
are.
Carl Jung

Old age though despised, is coveted by all.
Proverb

The belief that youth is the happiest time of life is
founded on a fallacy. The happiest person is the person
who thinks the most interesting thoughts and we grow
happier as we grow older.
William Lyon Phelps

SOME FOODS HAVE BEEN PROVEN TO
CONTRIBUTE TO A HEALTHY, AGEING BRAIN.
TOP OF THE LIST OF BRAIN FOODS IS SALMON.
WILD-CAUGHT SALMON HAS BEEN SHOWN
TO REDUCE DEPRESSION AND IMPROVE
CARDIOVASCULAR HEALTH. THERE IS ALSO
EVIDENCE THAT IT CAN HELP REDUCE THE RISK
OF STROKE AND DEMENTIA.

DID YOU KNOW?

By the time a person reaches 70 years old, he or she will have consumed over 12,000 gallons of water.

If you think forgetfulness is the sign of diminishing brainpower, think again. New research suggests that older people are slow on memory tests because they have more mental data to sift through to get to the answer.

At age 70, a person needs 500 fewer calories per day to maintain body weight.

70 THINGS YOU SHOULD KNOW BY THE TIME YOU TURN 70 (PART 5)

- Let it be
- How to take life as it comes
- Not to dwell on the negative
- Dreams don't have an expiry date
- How to make time for what matters
- Relax - nothing is as important as it seems at first
- Take the scenic route
- How to let go of the past

TO BE A GRACIOUS LOSER...

...AND A MAGNANIMOUS WINNER

EDMOND HOYLE IS CONSIDERED TO BE THE WORLD'S FIRST TECHNICAL WRITER ON THE RULES OF CARD GAMES. HE WAS 70 WHEN HE FIRST BEGAN RECORDING THE RULES OF VARIOUS CARD GAMES.

YOU'RE NEVER TOO OLD

Anna Mary Robertson Moses, better known as Grandma Moses, began her prolific painting career aged 78.

Groucho Marx played God in the movie Skidoo at the age of 77.

Benjamin Franklin signed the Declaration of Independence when he was 70.

At the age of 75, Japanese ukiyo-e painter Katsushika Hokusai produced the significant landscape series 'One Hundred Views of Mount Fuji'.

THINGS TO DO NOW YOU'RE 70

- Indulge in gardening
- Learn to cook a new dish
- Sponsor a child
- Explore the world
- Throw yourself a birthday party
- Pass on life lessons
- Spend more time with family and friends
- Volunteer for a charity
- Learn to enjoy your own company

RIDE IN A HOT AIR BALLOON

WE DO NOT COUNT A MAN'S YEARS UNTIL HE HAS NOTHING ELSE TO COUNT.

RALPH WALDO EMERSON

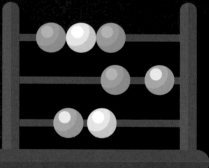

A WORD FROM THE WISE

It is not by muscle, speed, or physical dexterity that great things are achieved, but by reflection, force of character, and judgment. In these qualities old age is usually not only not poorer, but is even richer.
Cicero

Another belief of mine: that everyone else my age is an adult, whereas I am merely in disguise.
Margaret Atwood

It's not how old you are, it's how you are old.
Jules Renard

Nothing is more enjoyable than a leisured old age.
Cicero

As for old age, embrace and love it. It abounds with pleasure if you know how to use it. The gradually declining years are among the sweetest in a man's life.
Seneca

THE AVERAGE TIME SPENT SLEEPING IS ESTIMATED TO TOTAL ABOUT 6 HOURS 40 MINUTES A NIGHT, SO THIS MEANS WE WILL SPEND ABOUT 22 YEARS, OR 192,848 HOURS, OF OUR LIFE ASLEEP.

DID YOU KNOW?

There are some physical gains to be had with ageing - you will sweat less, for one! Shrinking sweat glands mean you can wave goodbye to embarrassing underarm sweat patches.

There's a species of jellyfish that cannot die of old age. After sexual maturity it ages backwards, going through reverse-puberty so it can start the cycle all over again. It can repeat this cycle indefinitely, making it biologically immortal!

Several studies have shown that pensioners who engage in regular light exercise - whether it's walking, dancing, pottering in the garden or washing the car - are two and a half times less vulnerable to developing severe long-term health problems than their less-active counterparts.

70 THINGS YOU SHOULD KNOW BY THE TIME YOU TURN 70 (PART 6)

- Money is overrated
- It's never too late to be happy
- Surround yourself with people you love
- Be patient
- How little you actually know
- Who you can trust
- Humour is a powerful life force
- How to be completely honest
- To listen more than you talk

LIFE HAS A RHYTHM... NOTHING EVER STAYS ALL BAD OR ALL GOOD

YOUNG PEOPLE KNOW HOW TO RUN FAST... BUT OLD PEOPLE KNOW THE WAY.

YOU'RE HAVING A LAUGH

Two elderly women were eating breakfast in a restaurant one morning. Ethel noticed something funny about Mabel's ear and she said, 'Mabel, did you know you've got a suppository in your left ear?' Mabel answered, 'I have? A suppository?' She pulled it out and stared at it. Then she said, 'Ethel, I'm glad you saw this thing. Now I think I know where my hearing aid is.'

Life would be infinitely happier if we could only be born at the age of eighty and gradually approach eighteen.
Mark Twain

Denunciation of the young is a necessary part of the hygiene of older people, and greatly assists the circulation of their blood.
Logan Pearsall Smith

NEVER RETIRE. MICHELANGELO WAS CARVING THE RONDANINI JUST BEFORE HE DIED AT 89. VERDI FINISHED HIS OPERA FALSTAFF AT 80. AND THE 80-YEAR-OLD SPANISH ARTIST GOYA SCRAWLED ON A DRAWING, 'I AM STILL LEARNING'.

DR W. GIFFORD-JONES

A WORD FROM THE WISE

I do not fear death. I had been dead for billions and billions of years before I was born, and had not suffered the slightest inconvenience from it.
Mark Twain

Nostalgia is a file that removes the rough edges from the good old days.
Doug Larson

To keep the heart unwrinkled, to be hopeful, kindly, cheerful, reverent that is to triumph over old age.
Thomas B. Aldrich

The tragedy of old age is not that one is old, but that one is young.
Oscar Wilde

Perhaps one has to be very old before one learns to be amused rather than shocked.
Pearl S. Buck

YOU'RE NEVER TOO OLD

Wallace Stevens won a Pulitzer Prize for his Collected Poems at the age of 76.

At the age of 73, Rex Harrison completed a successful 11-month tour in My Fair Lady.

70-year-old marathon runner Judy Brenner claimed she was just being a good citizen when she chased a young shoplifter 100 feet and held on to him until the police arrived.

At 70 years old, Golda Meir became the 4th prime minister of Israel.

AT THE AGE OF 76, H. G. WELLS COMPLETED HIS DOCTORAL DISSERTATION, EARNING A D.SC. FROM LONDON UNIVERSITY. HE HAD DROPPED OUT OF SCHOOL WHEN HE WAS 14.

70 THINGS YOU SHOULD KNOW BY THE TIME YOU TURN 70 (PART 7)

- Where your talents are best utilised
- How to distinguish your needs from your wants
- How to comfort others
- How to find something comical in every situation
- To give people a second chance...but not a third
- Say sorry
- You aren't always right
- Never to eat oysters in months without an 'r'
- To embrace your age

HOW TO
TELL JOKES

THINGS TO DO NOW YOU'RE 70

- Plant trees

- Make new friends

- Go south for the winter

- Study for a degree

- Reclaim an old passion

- Consider part-time work

- Visit art galleries

- Write a memoir

- Do that thing you've been putting off for years

GO
SCUBA DIVING

50s & 60s TRIVIA
(PART 4)

1. Who delivered the famous speech 'I Have a Dream' in August of 1963?

2. In 1964, the Sunday Times in the United Kingdom became the first paper to print a what?

3. Who is the author of the classic novel Catch-22, first published in 1961

4. Which Beatles song did Ella Fitzgerald take into the 1964 UK charts?

5. What new type of telephone was invented in 1963?

6. What did Elvis Presley receive from the US army in 1960?

7. Who originally sang 'That'll Be the Day' in 1957?

8. In 1961, which record became Chubby Checker's first UK top 30 hit?

9. Yuri Gagarin became the first man in space in April 1961, what was the name of the craft?

10. Which English pirate radio station was founded by Ronan O'Rahilly in 1964?

(See page 96 for answers)

YOU'RE NEVER TOO OLD

General Douglas MacArthur was given command of the United Nations' army in the Korean War when he was 70.

Louise Bourgeois wasn't featured in the Museum of Modern Art until she was 71.

Alexander Graham Bell received a patent for work he was doing on a hydrofoil boat at the age of 75.

Winston Churchill was 79 when he received the Nobel Prize for Literature 'for his mastery of historical and biographical description as well as for brilliant oratory in defending exalted human values.'

AGED 77, JOHN GLENN BECAME THE OLDEST PERSON TO GO INTO SPACE.

WHEN I FEAR THE LOSS OF MY YOUTHFULNESS AND REFUSE TO ACCEPT THE REALITY OF AGEING, I TURN MY FACE TO THE BRILLIANT COLORS OF AUTUMN TREES.

JOYCE RUPP & MACRINA WIEDERKEHR

A WORD FROM THE WISE

It is not by the gray of the hair that one knows the age of the heart.
Edward G. Bulwer-Lytton

Old age is like climbing a mountain. You climb from ledge to ledge. The higher you get, the more tired and restless you become, but your view becomes more extensive.
Ingmar Bergman

Cherish youth but trust old age.
Proverb

Old age has its pleasures, which, though different, are not less than the pleasures of youth.
W. Somerset Maugham

How did it get so late so soon?
Dr Seuss

ANSWERS: 50s & 60s TRIVIA

(PART 1)

1. Prime Minister Harold Macmillan

2. Anthony Perkins

3. 'Return to Sender'

4. Nuclear weapons

5. Frank Sinatra, Dean Martin, Sammy Davis Jr, Joey Bishop and Peter Lawford

6. Barbie doll

7. Game of Life

8. John F. Kennedy

9. 'Heartbreak Hotel'

10. Jersey

(PART 2)

(PART 3)

5. 'Glad All Over'

6. Habitat

7. The Suez Canal

8. The Yardbirds

9. Marilyn Monroe

10. David Lean

(PART 4)

1. Martin Luther King Jr

2. A colour supplement

3. Joseph Heller

4. 'Can't Buy Me Love'

5. Touch-tone

6. Honorable discharge

7. Buddy Holly & The Crickets

8. 'Pony Time'

9. Vostok 1

10. Radio Caroline